Musical Instruments A-Z

Written & Illustrated by Melissa Crosson

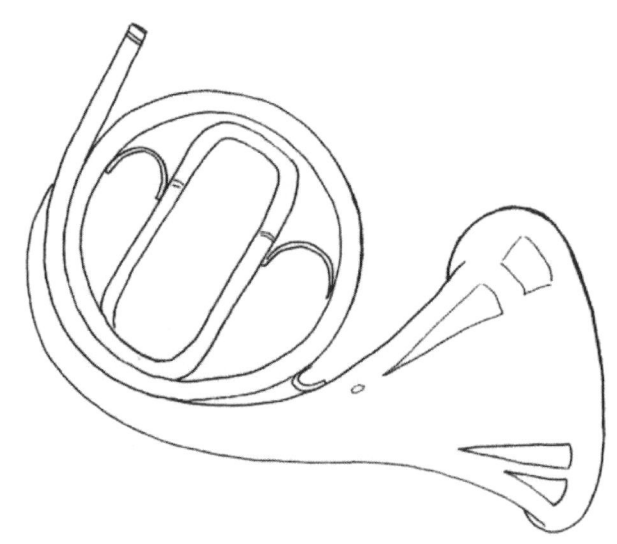
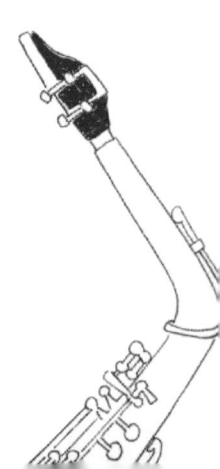

Many thanks and much appreciation goes out to all the people that taught me art and those that support me during my artistic journey. Thank you to my art teachers Sue Johnson, Karen Parker, Don Moore, and Marvin Espy. Thank you Foothills Painters, ArtPop Street Gallery, and other artist friends for inspiring me. Thank you to my parents for bringing me in this world and introducing me to musical instruments. Thank you to my sisters Katie and Christina for your great taste in music. Thank you to my daughter Zoe Charlotte, my best creation, for cheering me on artistically and giving me time to create. Thank you to my love Christopher, who is my number one fan and listens to all my crazy ideas. Thank you to those who helped support me in the creation of this book. Lastly, thank you to my dear friends Beth and Eve who love to boogie down to great tunes. I am forever grateful.

Greetings kiddos and music lovers! Welcome to the whimsical world of musical instruments! Today we will explore musical instruments A to Z! So sit back, relax, and enjoy your musical journey!

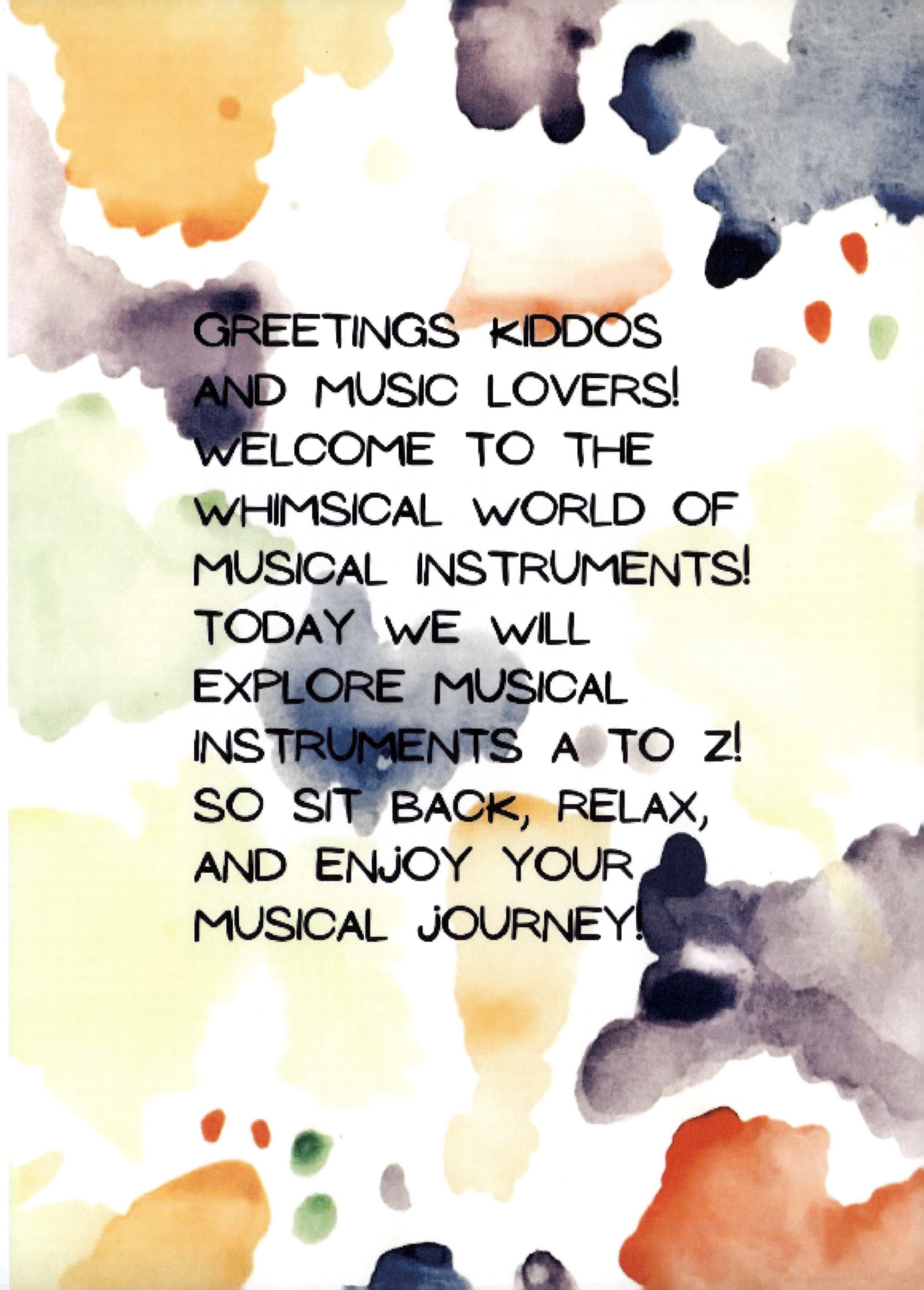

Accordion

Banjo

Clarinet

Drum

Electric Guitar

Flute

Guitar

Harmonica

Ikembe

Jug

Kazoo

Lyre

Mandolin

Natural Horn

Oboe

Piano

Quiribillo

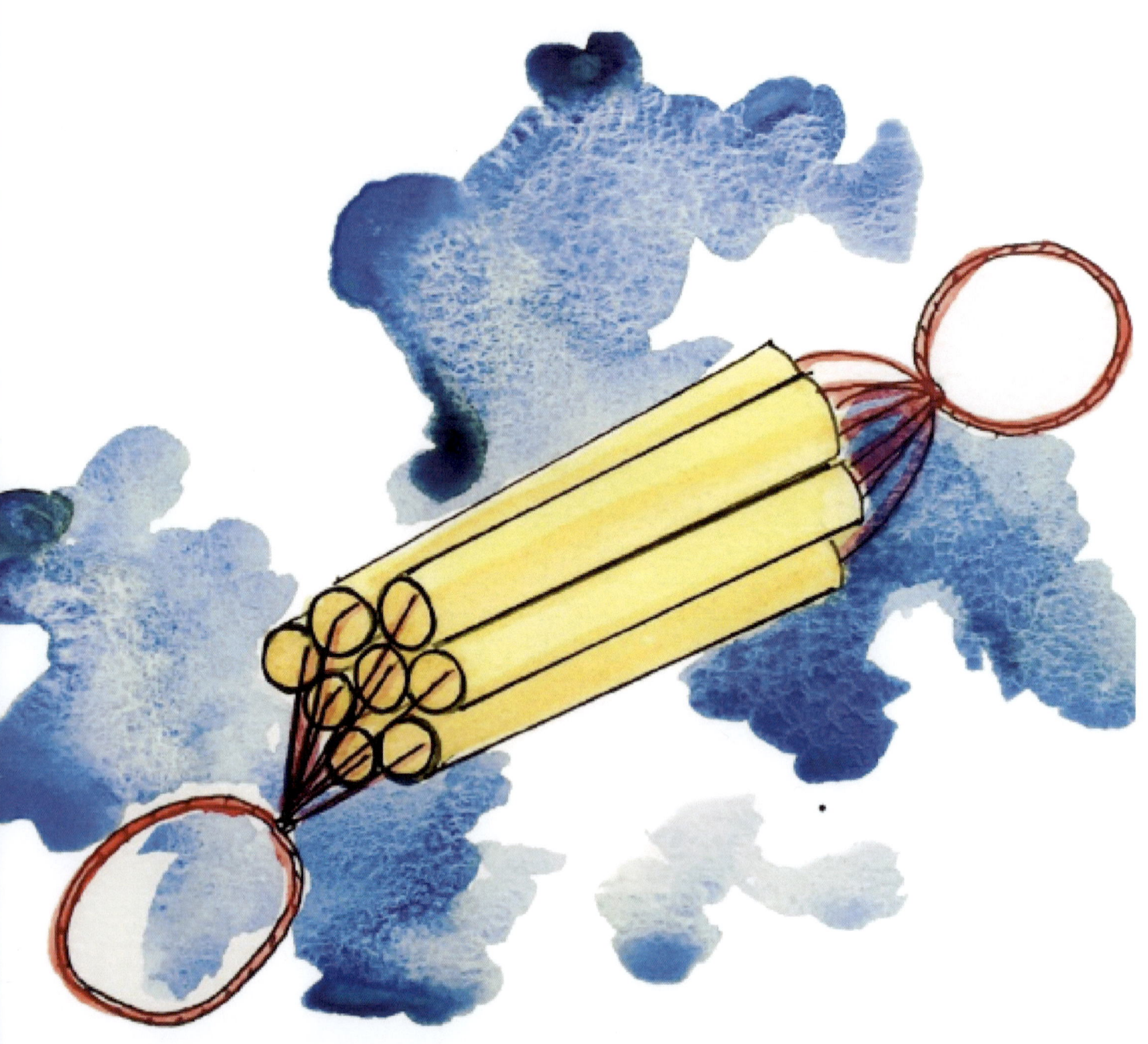

Recorder

Saxophone

Tambourine

Ukulele

Vibraslap

Washboard

Xylophone

Yehu

Zamponga

Musical Instruments A-Z Coloring Book

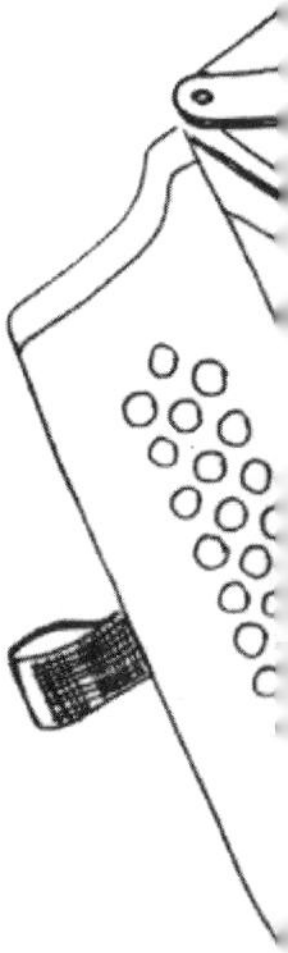

Written & Illustrated by Melissa Crosson

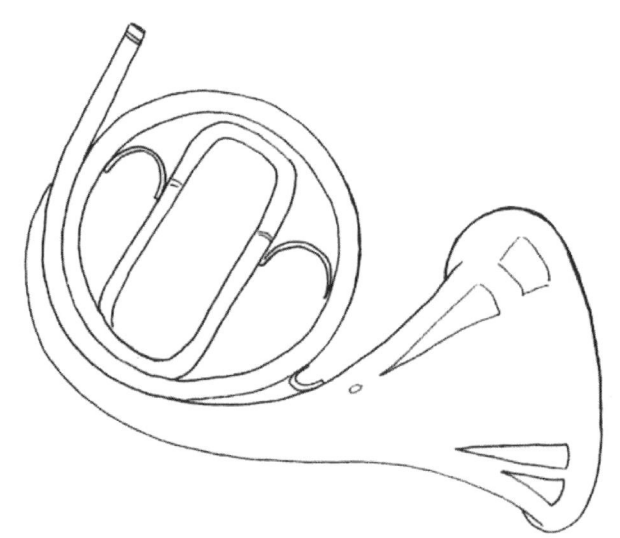
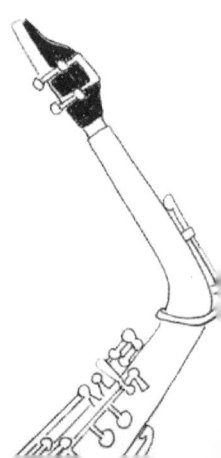

Accordion

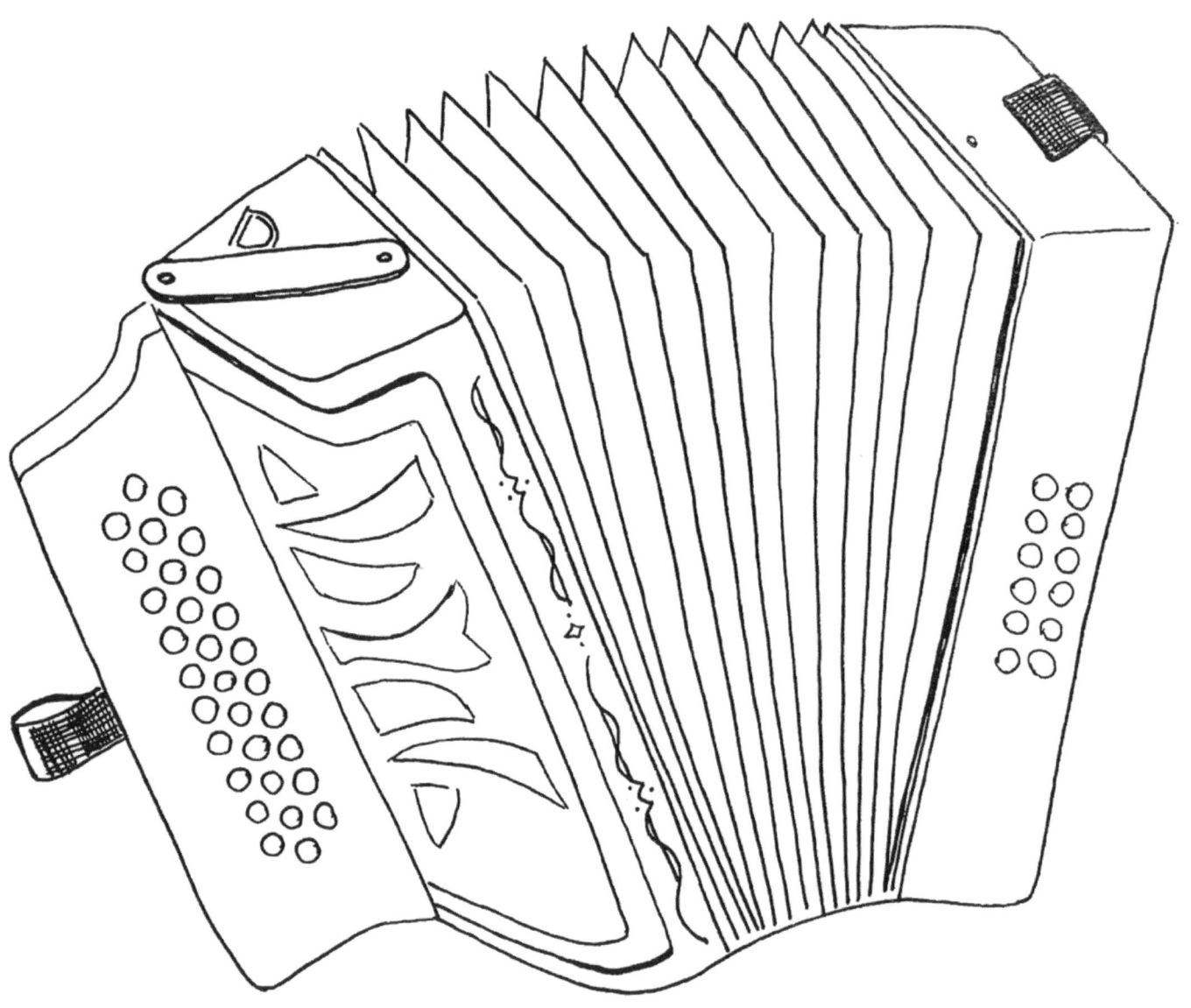

Banjo

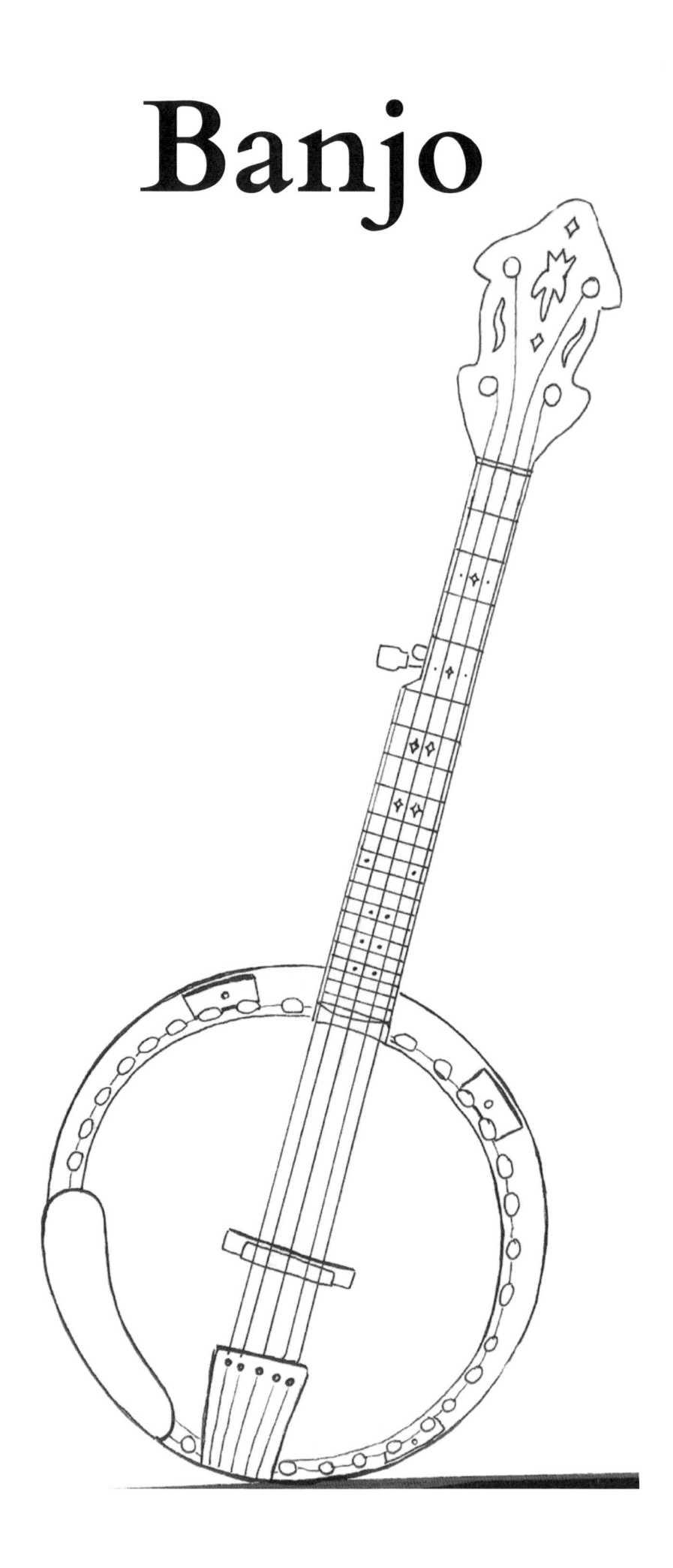

Clarinet

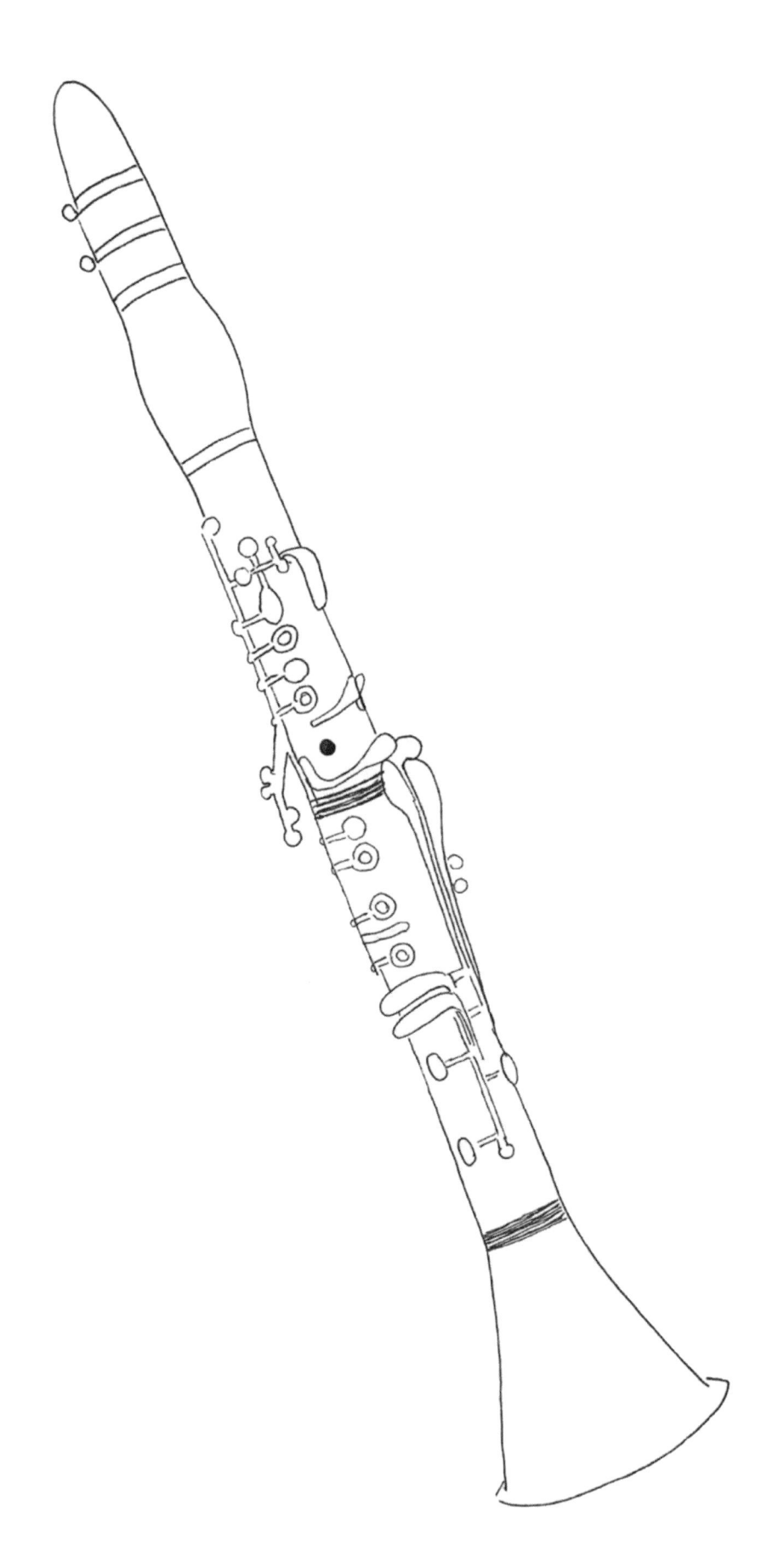

Drum

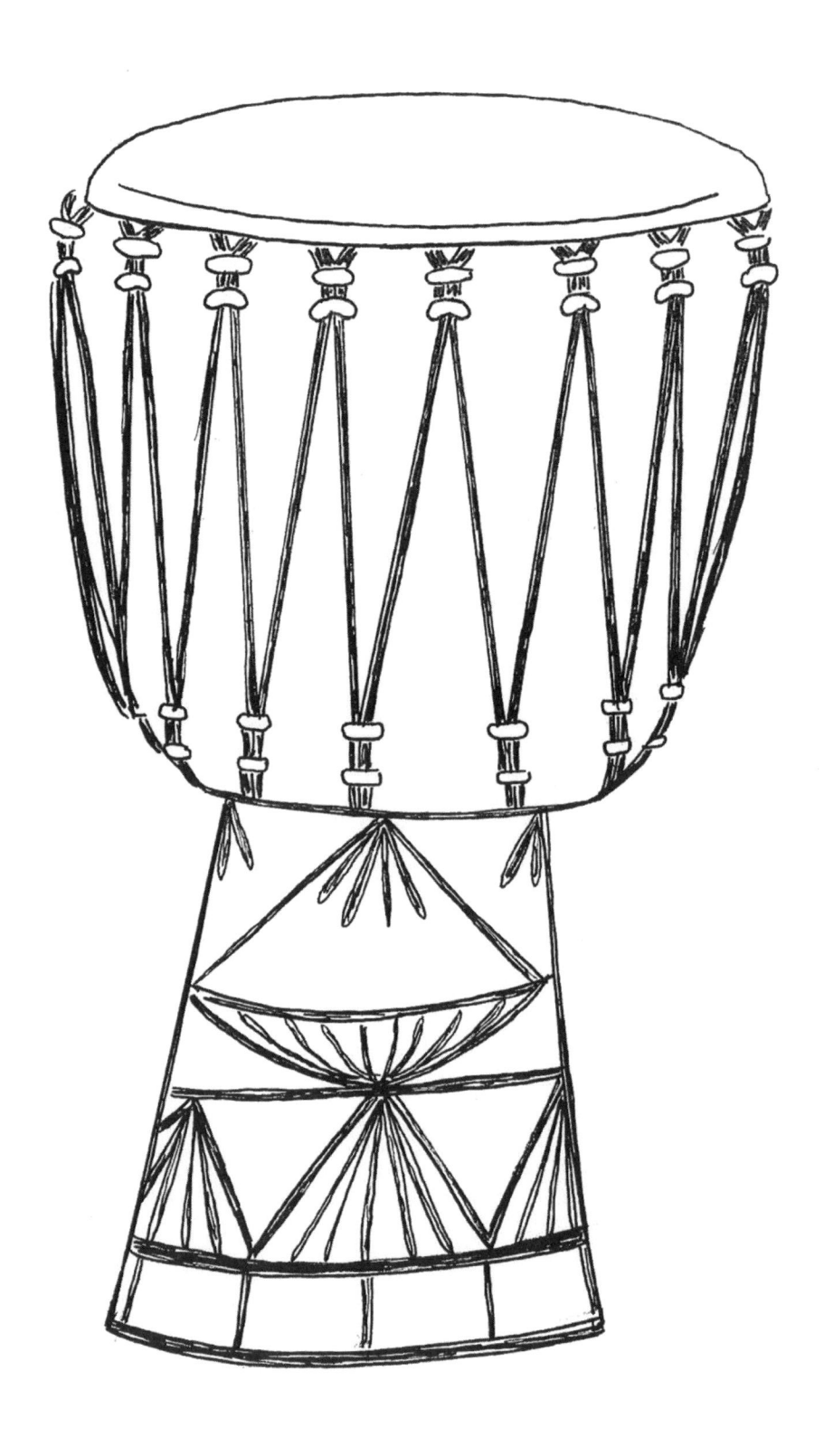

Electric Guitar

Flute

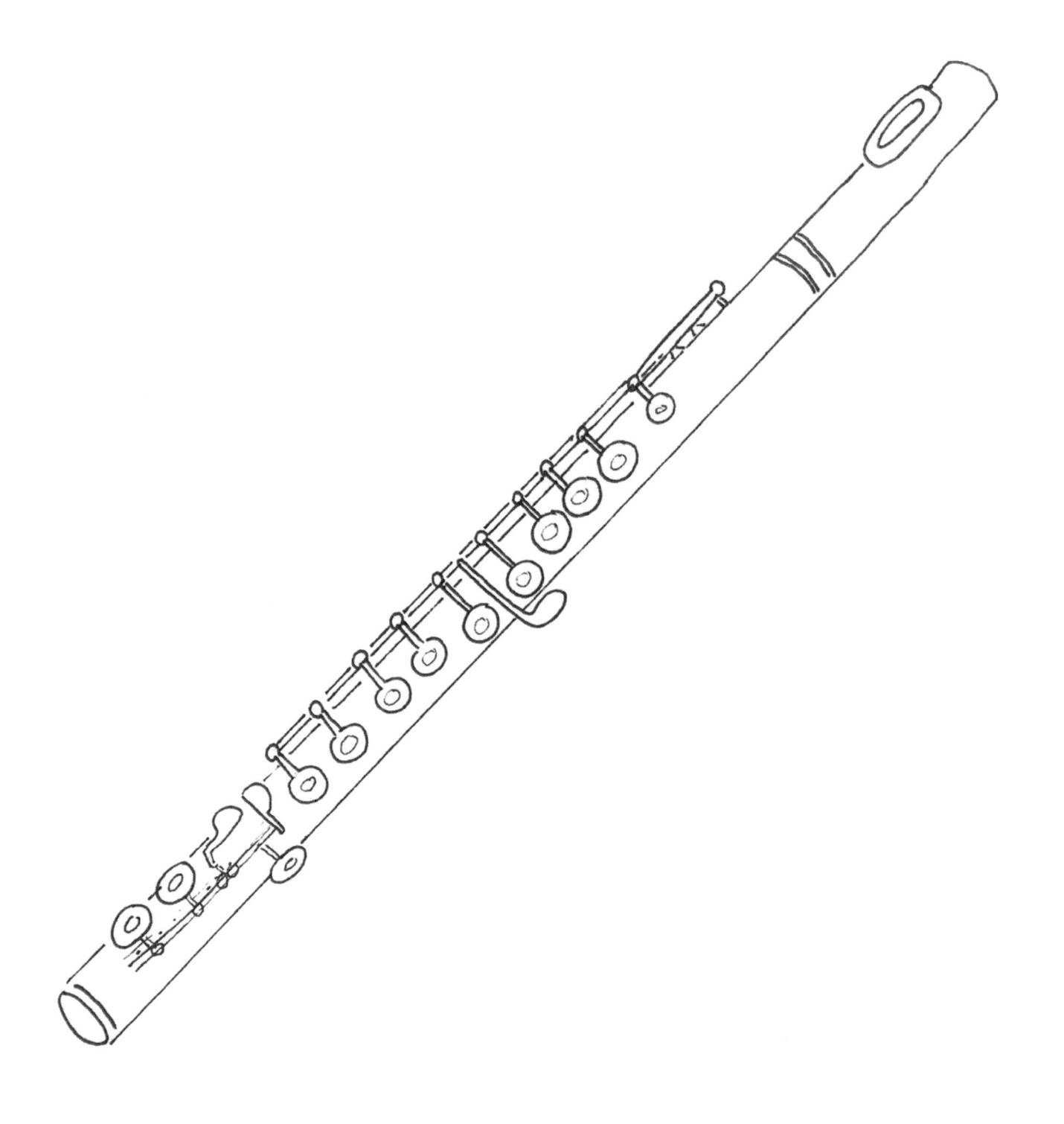

Guitar

Harmonica

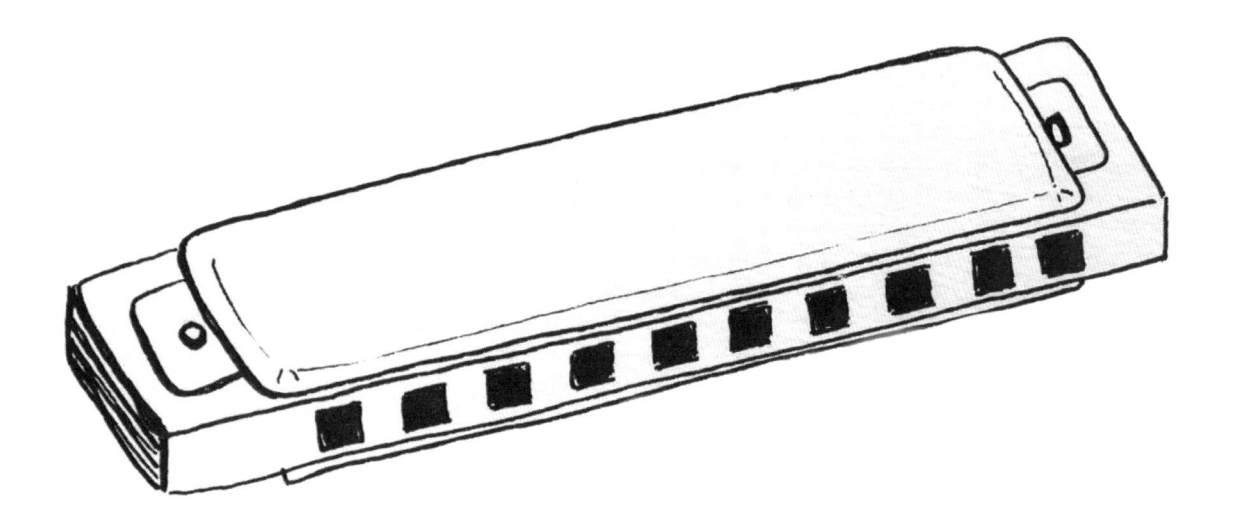

Ikembe

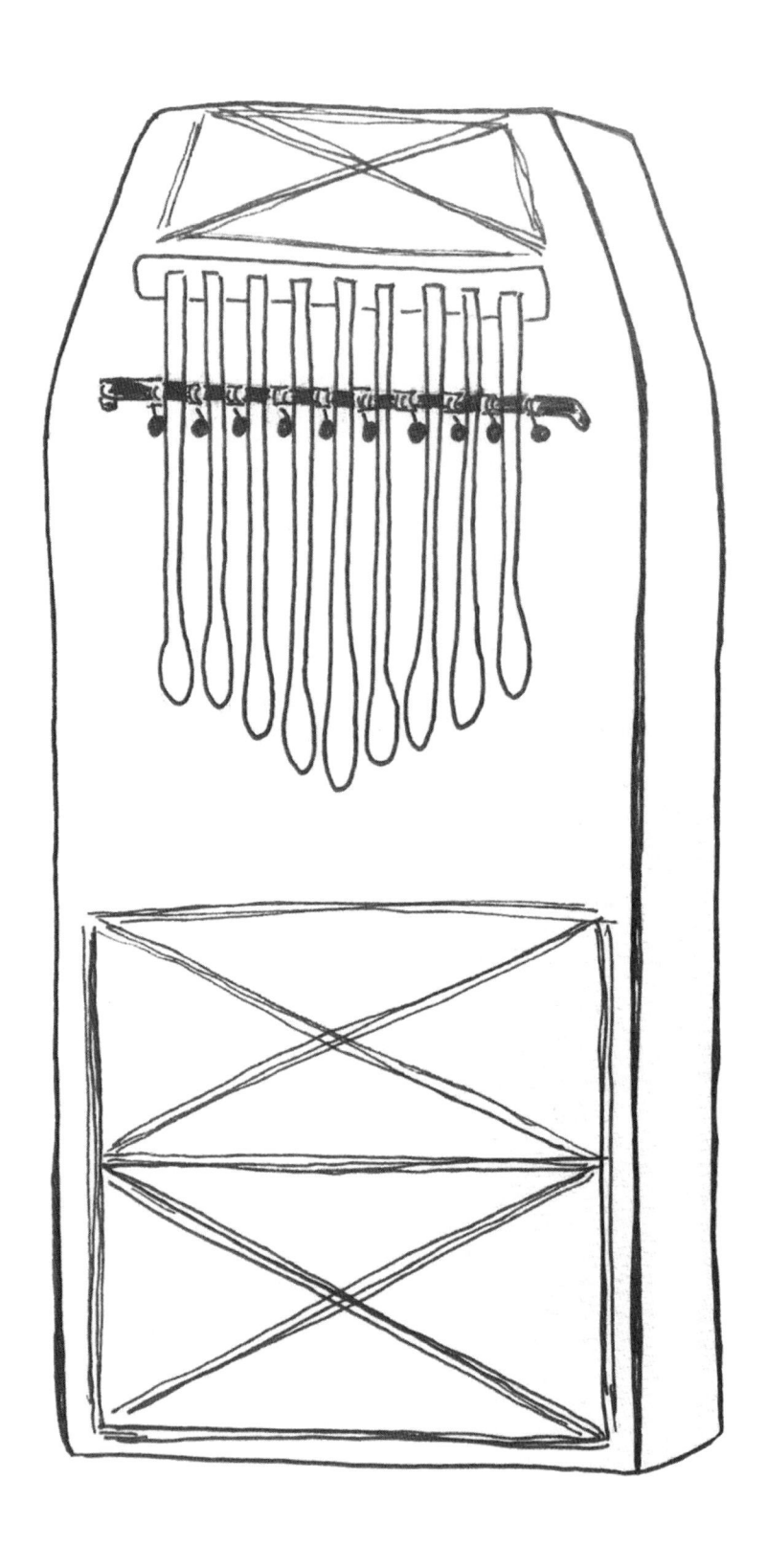

Jug

Kazoo

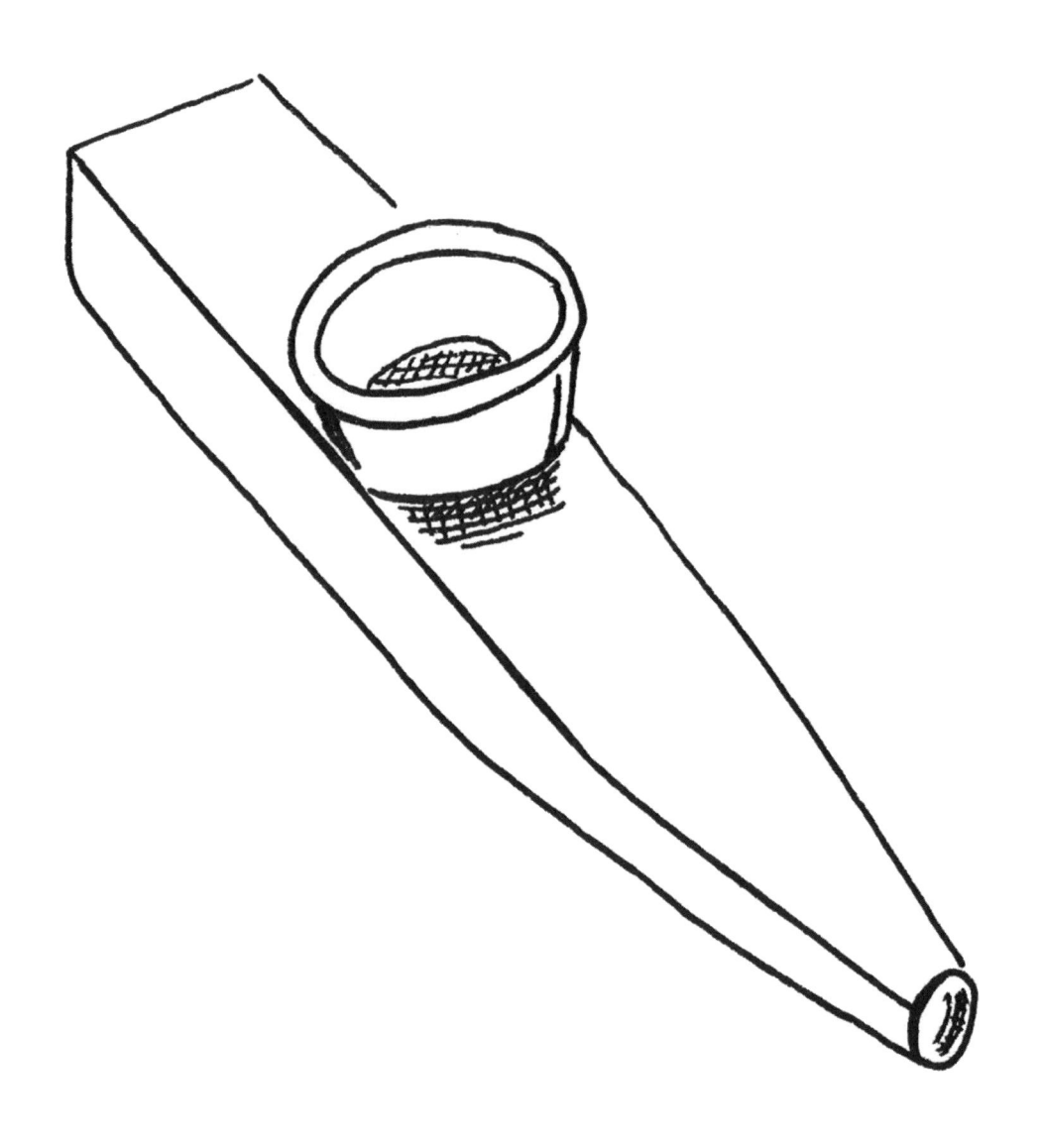

Lyre

Mandolin

Natural Horn

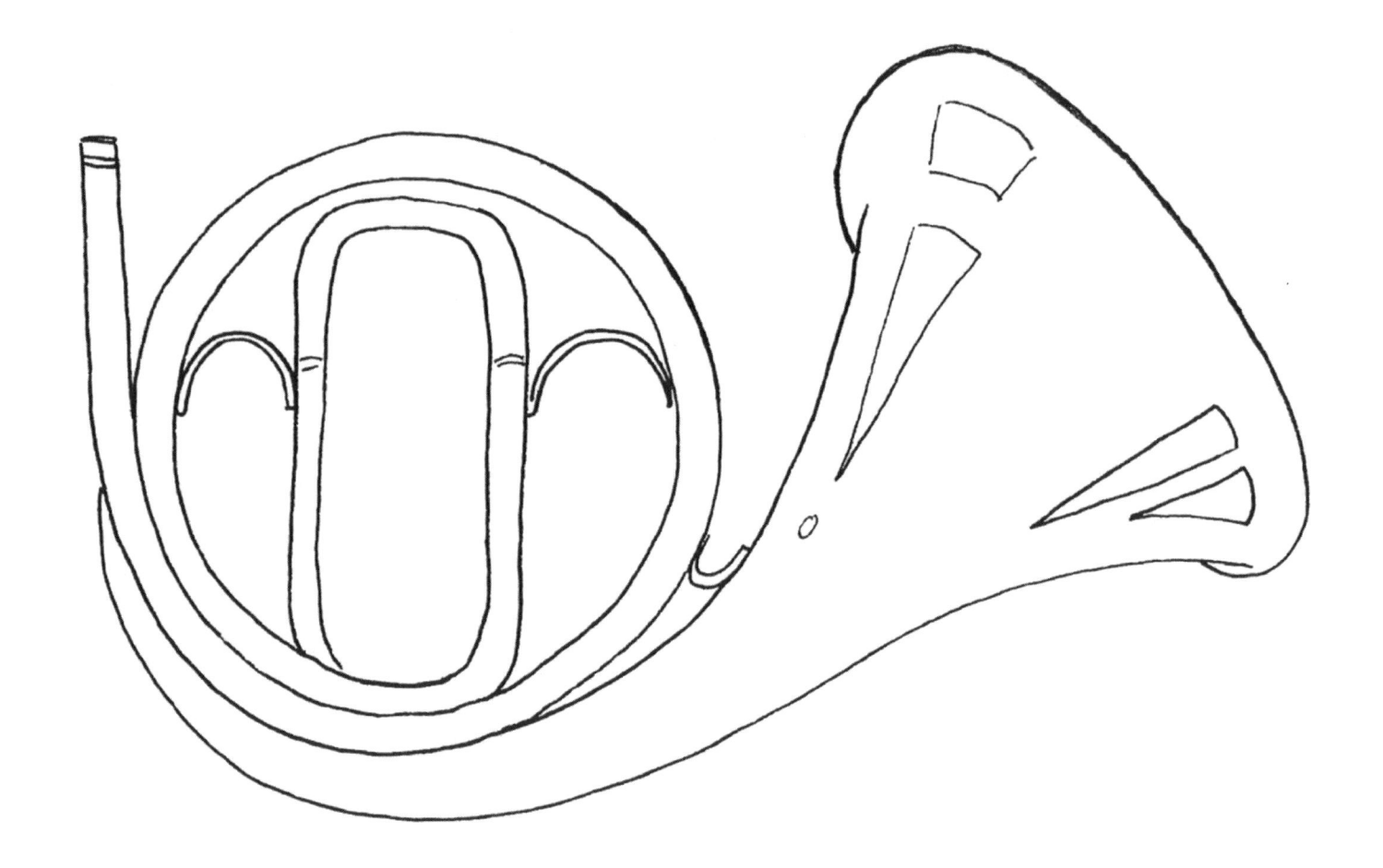

Oboe

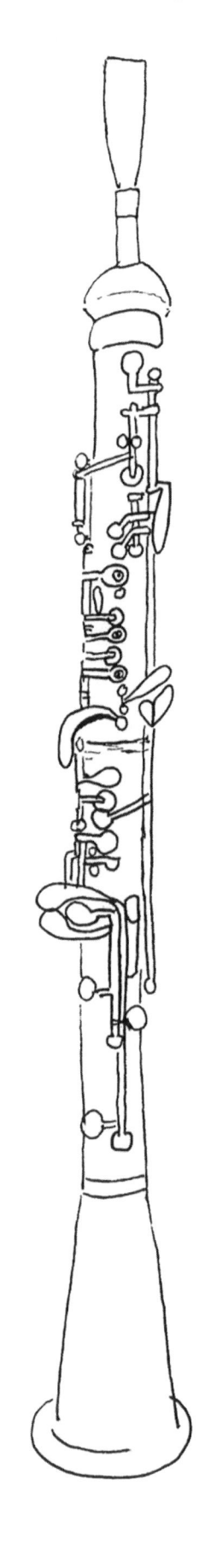

Piano

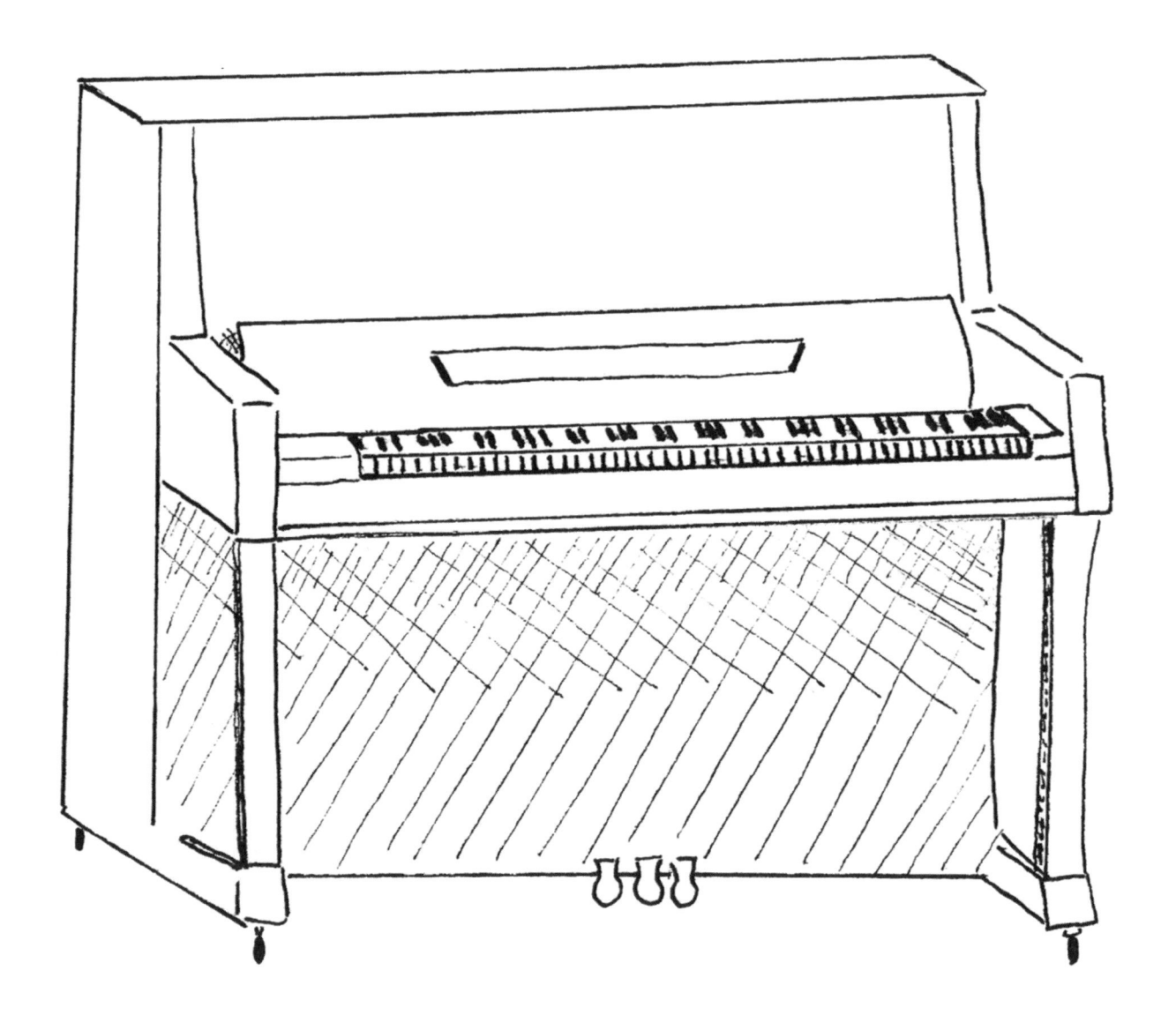

Quiribillo

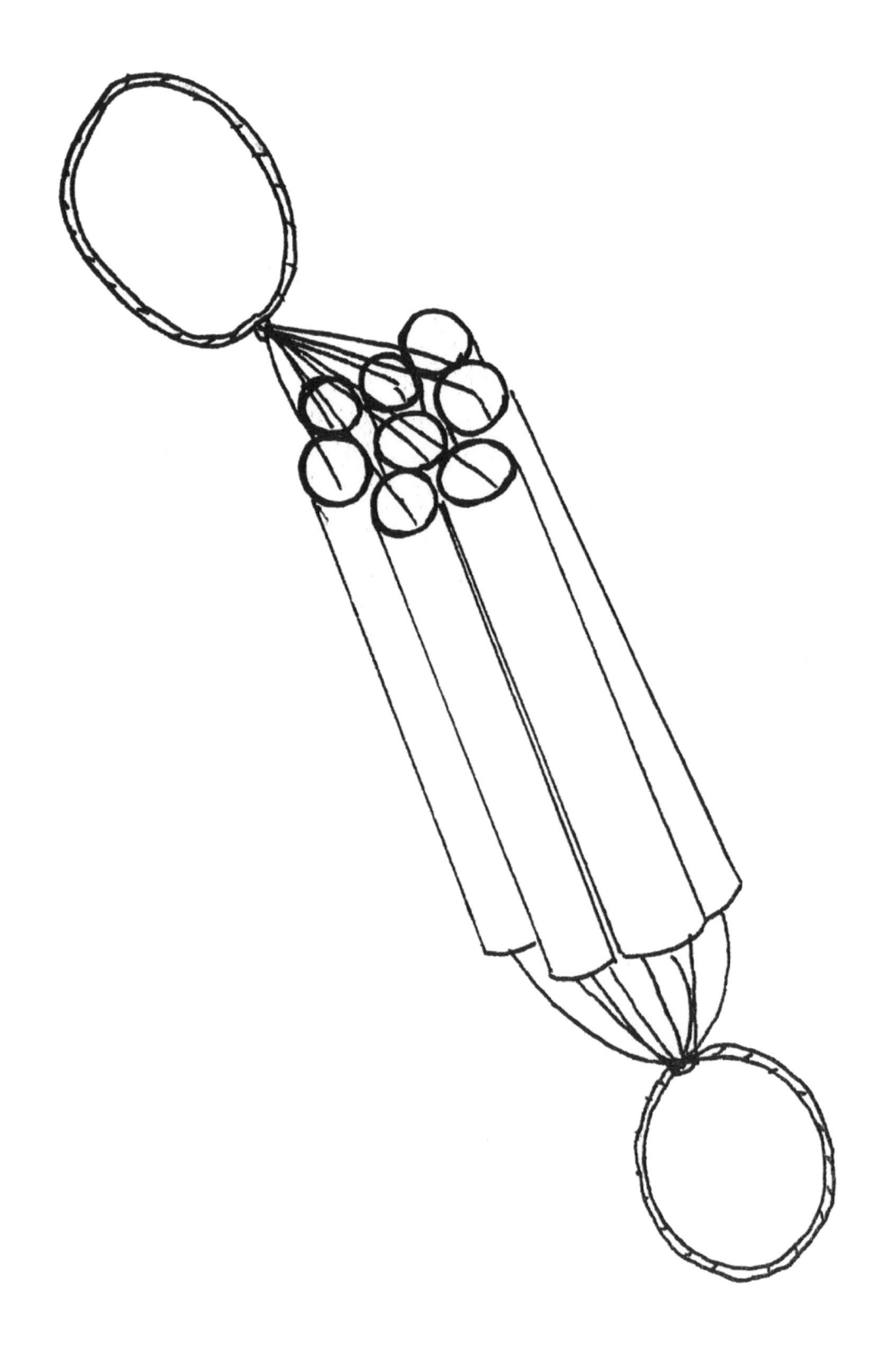

Recorder

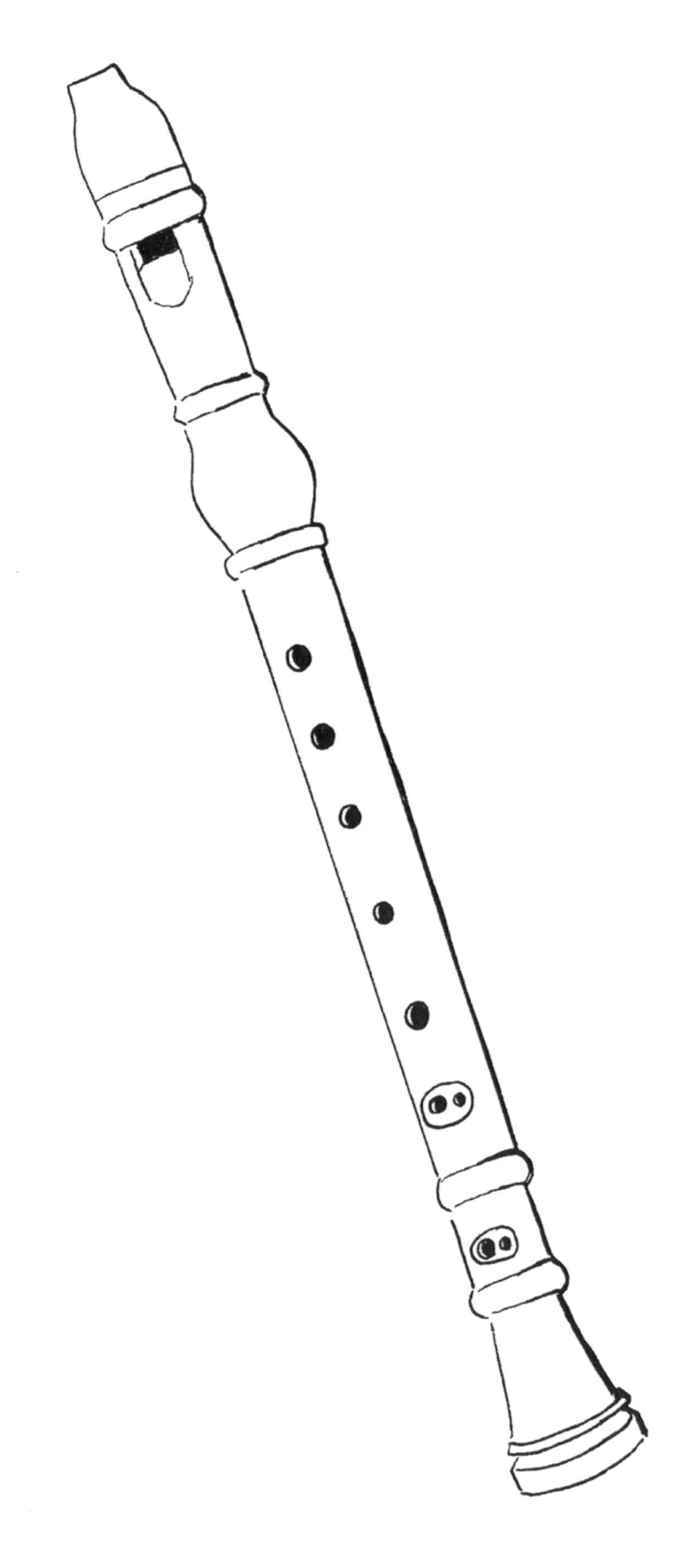

Saxophone

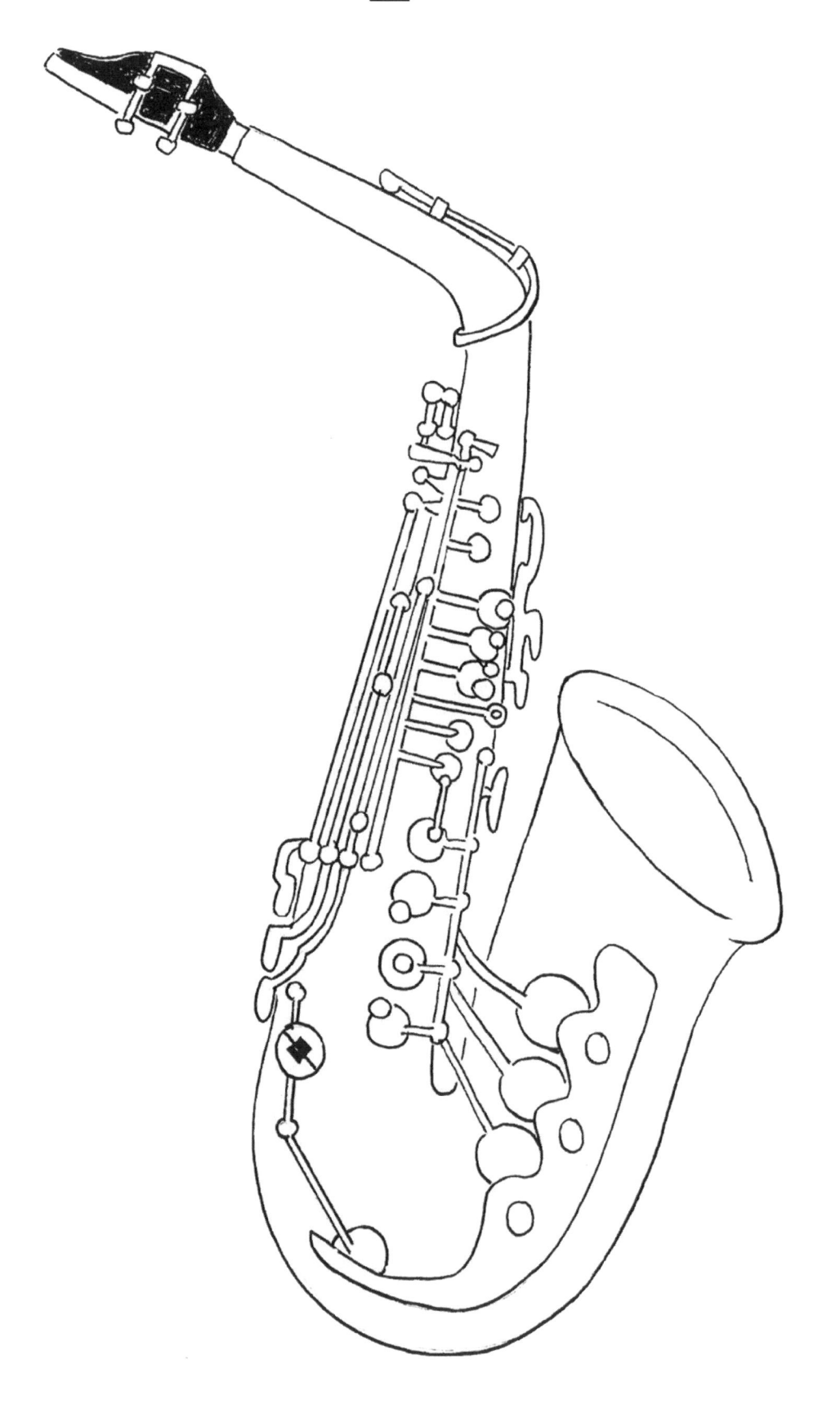

Tambourine

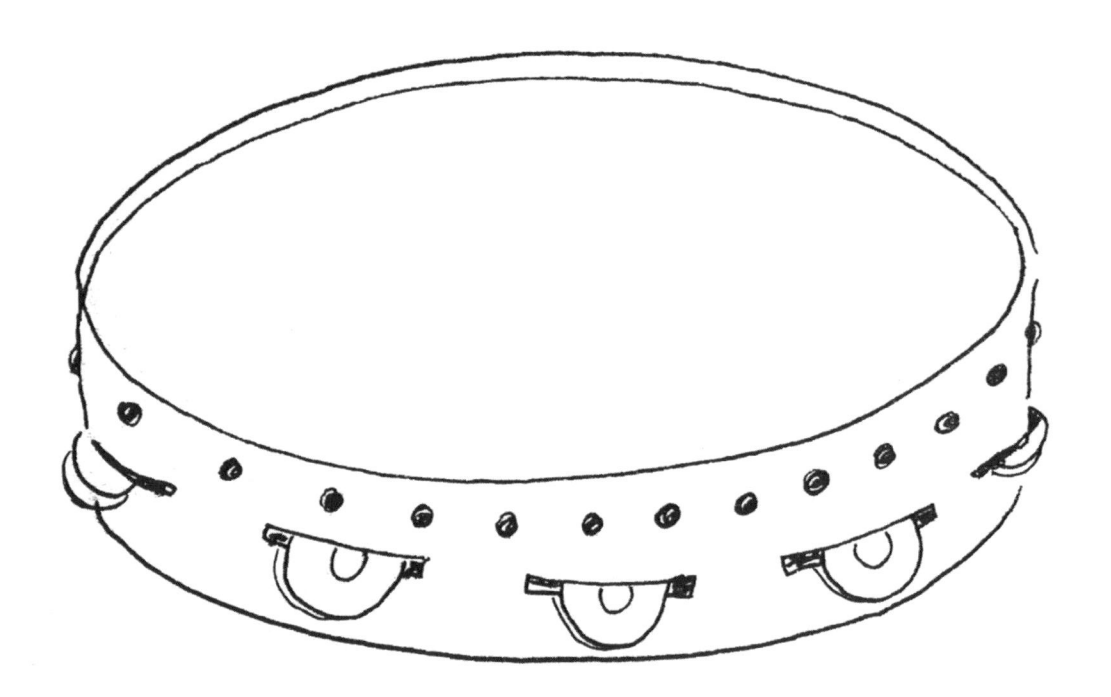

Ukulele

Vibraslap

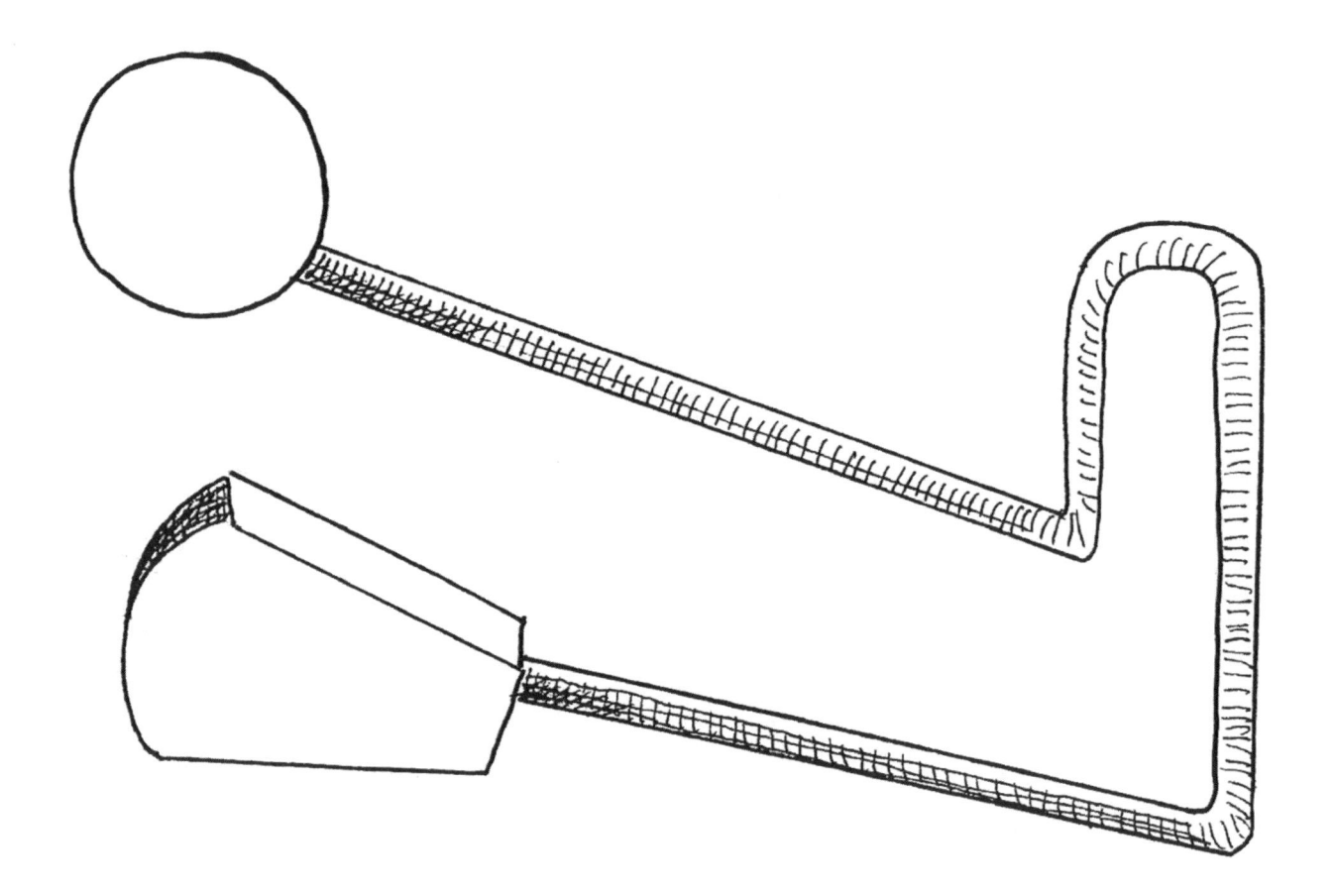

Washboard

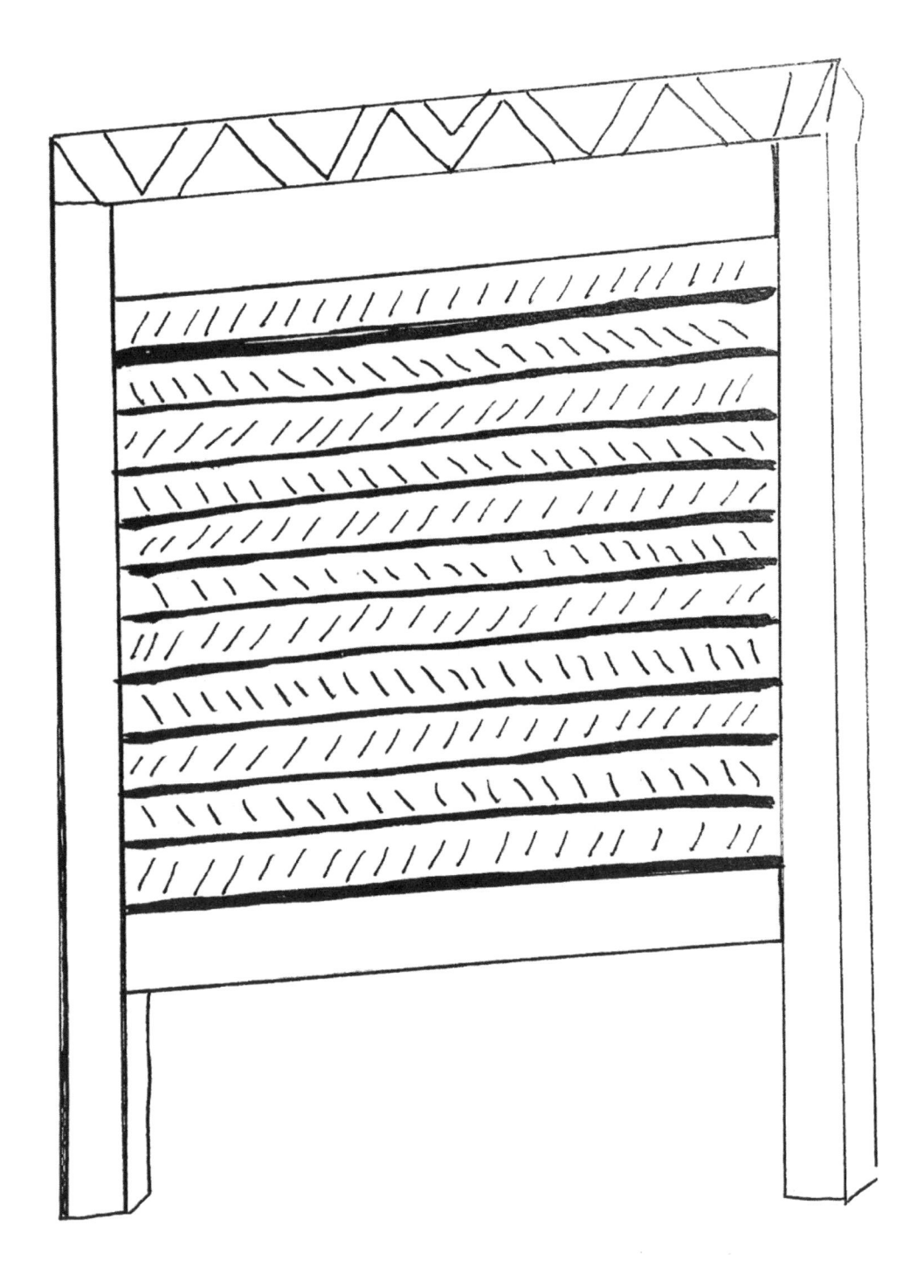

Xylophone

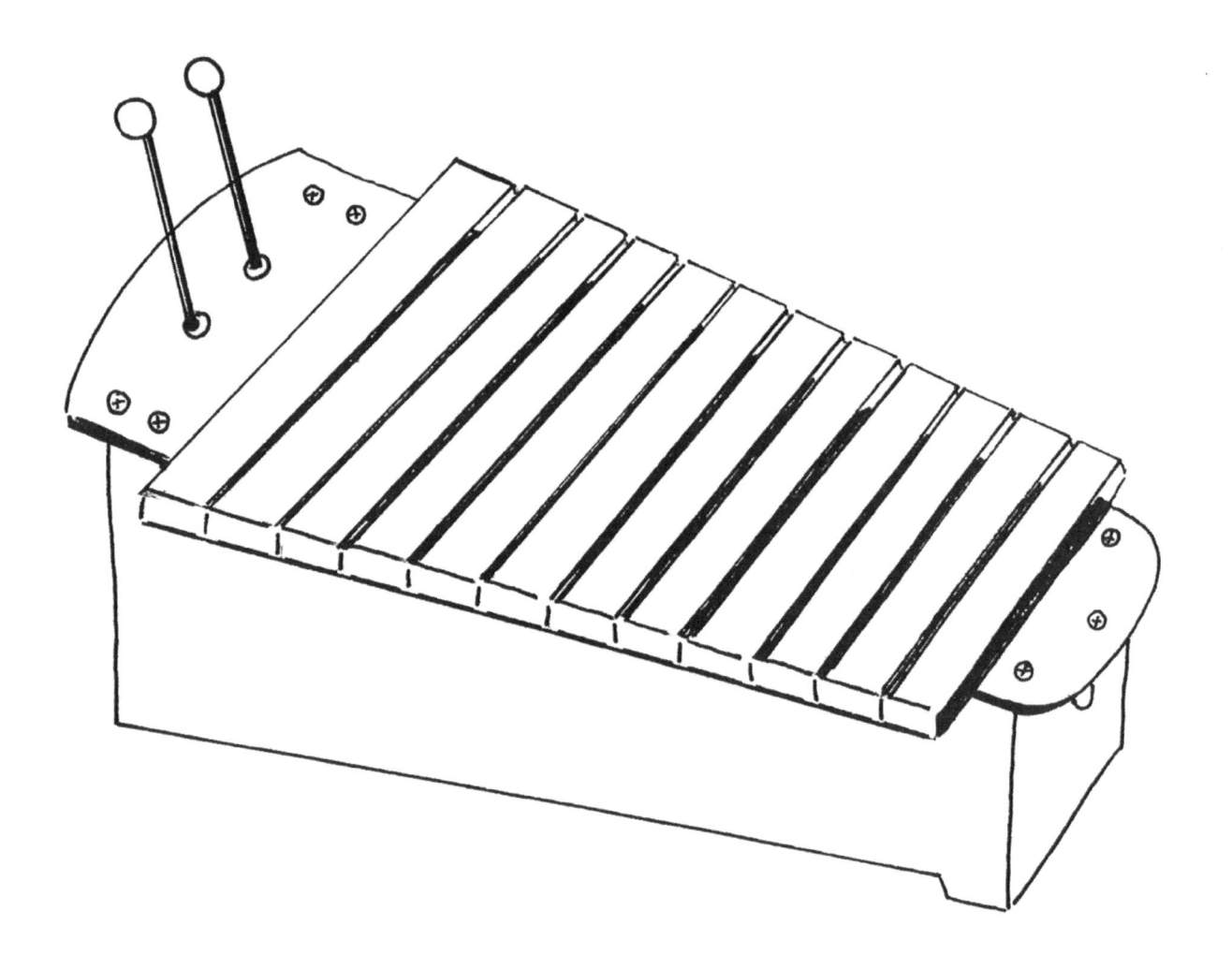

Yehu

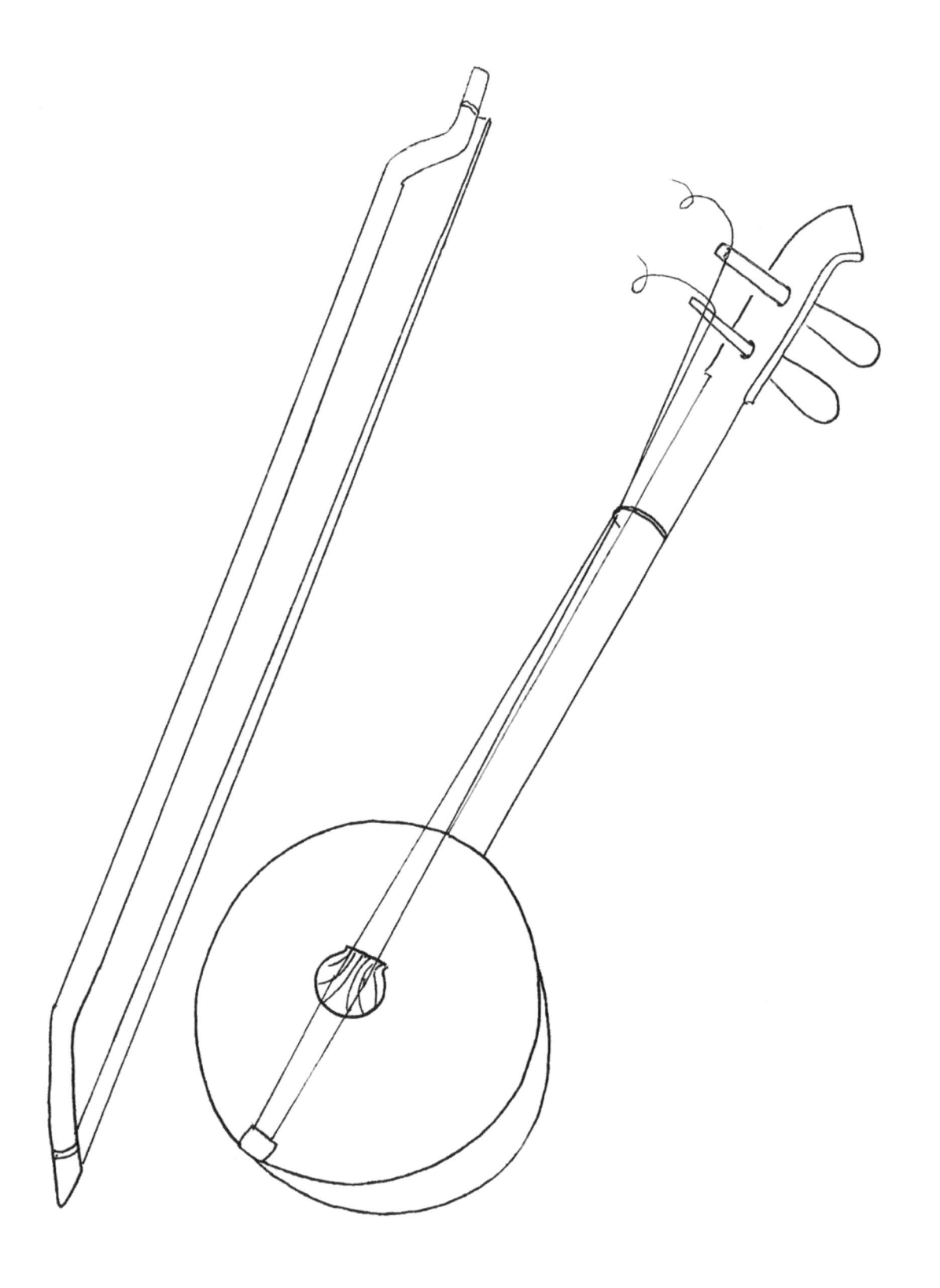

Zamponga

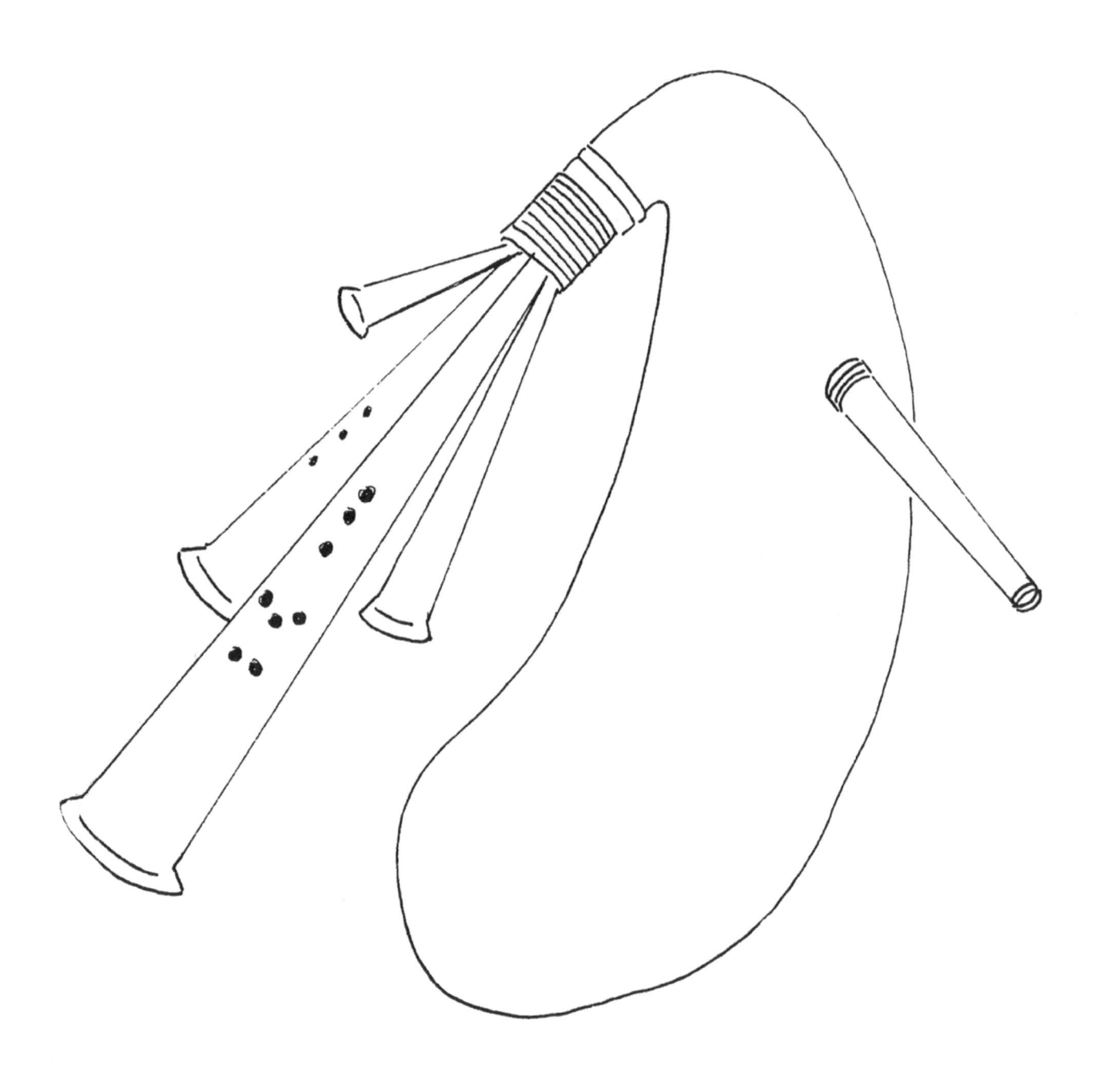

Melissa is a mom, artist, and friend who lives nestled in the foothills of Hickory, NC. She enjoys painting, gardening, and dancing in her spare time. Melissa spent years in the field of educating young children and decided to combine her love of teaching and art to create this book. Hopefully this will be one of many books to come.

Printed in Poland
by Amazon Fulfillment
Poland Sp. z o.o., Wrocław
17 June 2024